Table of Conte

Peter **Music** Publishing - All Rights Reserved **2021**

1. NOTE AND KEYS MARKINGS

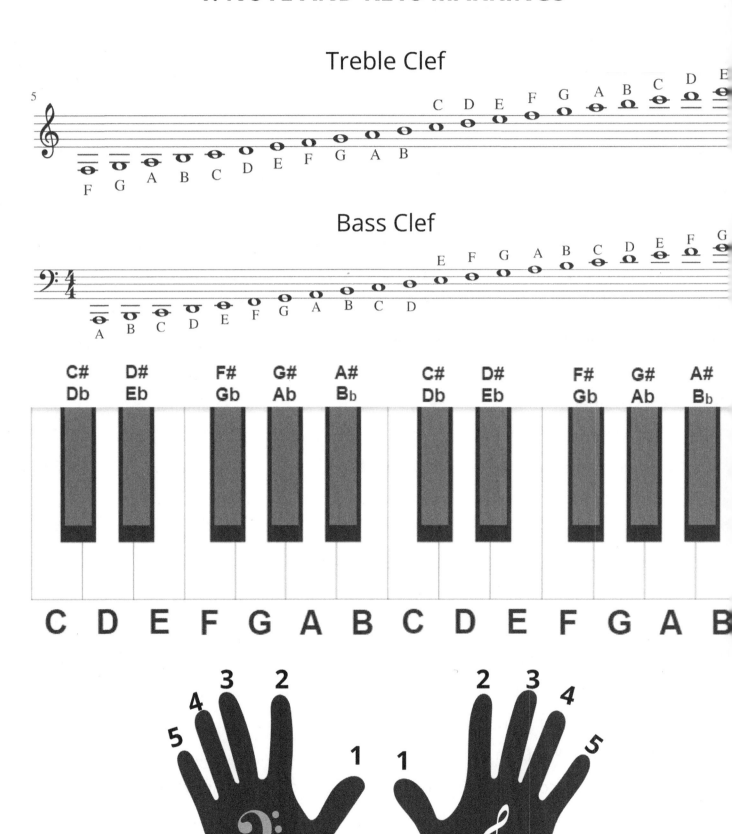

2. ACCOMPANIMENT THEORY

Accompaniment is an integral part of music that supports and complements the main melody, vocals, or improvisation. It is often used by instruments such as piano, guitar, or drums and can be improvised or pre-written. Accompaniment can be divided into different types, such as chordal accompaniment, basic accompaniment, and figuration accompaniment.

Chordal Accompaniment - is built using various types of chords that provide a harmonic background for the melody.

Basic Accompaniment - typically consists of two notes played at an octave interval, and additional notes may be added to achieve a fuller sound.

Figuration Accompaniment - utilizes arpeggios, which are broken chords played melodically over time.

This book will show you accompaniment in the 3 most popular meters: **2/4, 3/4**, and **4/4.** Practicing different accompaniment patterns can help musicians improve their playing technique and ability to match the appropriate accompaniment to the style of their favorite songs. However, before we dive into the accompaniment styles, I would like you to practice all the exercises included in this book with me.

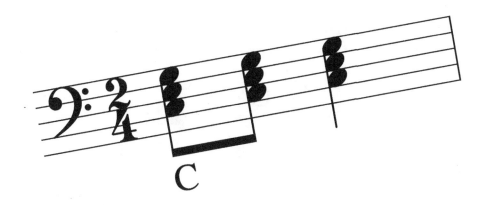

C

3. CIRCLE OF FIFTH IN PRACTICE

The circle of fifths and circle of fourths are musical tools used to explore the relationships between key signatures.

The circle of fifths is a graphical representation of all key signatures with sharps and flats. The notes are arranged in a circle in such a way that each note is connected to another note a perfect fifth away when moving clockwise, or a perfect fourth away when moving counterclockwise.

The circle of fifths enables musicians to easily discover the connections between notes in a specific key signature, making composition, improvisation, and chord progression creation easier.

Both circles are valuable in the composition and improvisation process as they help musicians understand which notes fit within a particular key signature and which do not. The circle of fifths particularly intriguing because it reveals the cyclical nature of the relationships between key signatures. For instance, when moving along the circle of fifths, we can observe that each subsequent key signature differs by one sharp or flat, which affects the sound and character of a composition. Thus, the circle of fifths serves not only as a practical tool but also as an inspiring source for musicians seeking new combinations of sounds and harmonic colors.

The diagram below represents major and minor key signatures with sharps and flats.

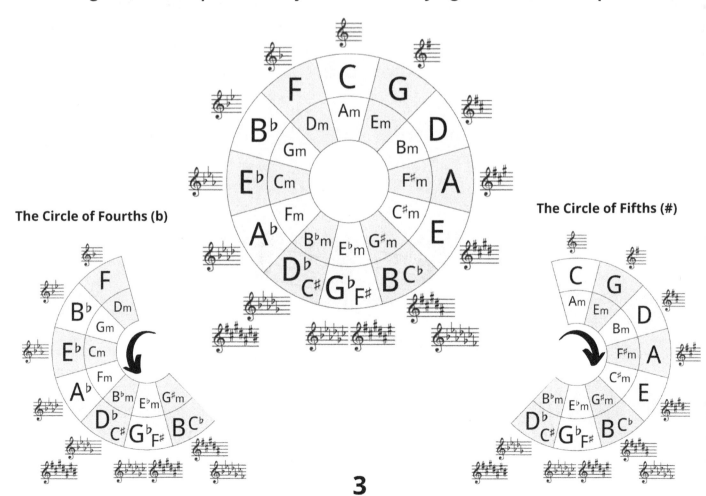

The Circle of Fourths (b)

The Circle of Fifths (#)

HOW TO UNDERSTAND AND READ "KEYS"

onations refer to sets of pitches that serve as the building blocks of specific musical scales. For example, the C major tonation consists of the pitches C-D-E-F-G-A-B-C, starting from the pitch indicated by the tonation. Each tonation has its own set of pitches, which is called a scale.

here are two types of tonations in music: sharp (#) tonation and flat (b) tonation. In practice, key signatures indicate which pitches on the staff should be raised (by a half step) or lowered (by a half step).

or example, the **D major** tonation has two sharps located on the fifth line (representing the itches F) and on the third space (representing the pitches C). These pitches need to be raised by a half step: "C" becomes "C#" and "F" becomes "F#". Another example is the **B major** tonation, hich has two flats in the key signature. This means that the pitches B and E need to be lowered y a half step and played as Bb and Eb.

nderstanding tonations and key signatures, which indicate which pitches on the staff should be aised or lowered, is essential for precise and unambiguous musical notation and performance.

Example:

The sharp symbol (#) is located on the fifth line, which is why the pitch F is raised to F#. The same applies to the pitch C, which becomes C#.

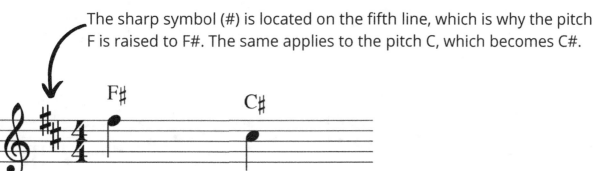

The flat symbol (b) is located on the fourth space, which is why the pitch E is lowered to Eb. The same applies to the pitch B, which becomes Bb.

* Each additional sharp or flat on the staff indicates that we are using more black keys.

4. <u>MAJOR</u> <u>SCALES</u> IN BOTH OCTAVES OF SHARP KEYS (LEFT HAND).

Piotr Tadrzyński

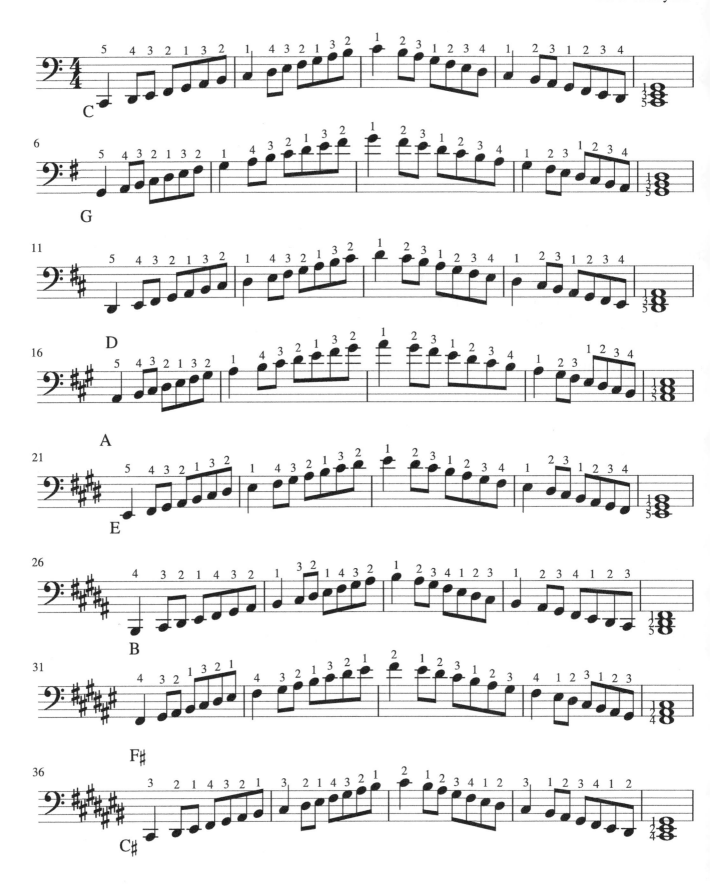

5

MAJOR SCALES IN BOTH OCTAVES OF FLAT KEYS (LEFT HAND).

MINOR SCALES IN BOTH OCTAVES OF SHARP KEYS (LEFT HAND).

Piotr Tadrzyńsk

MINOR SCALES IN BOTH OCTAVES OF FLAT KEYS (LEFT HAND).

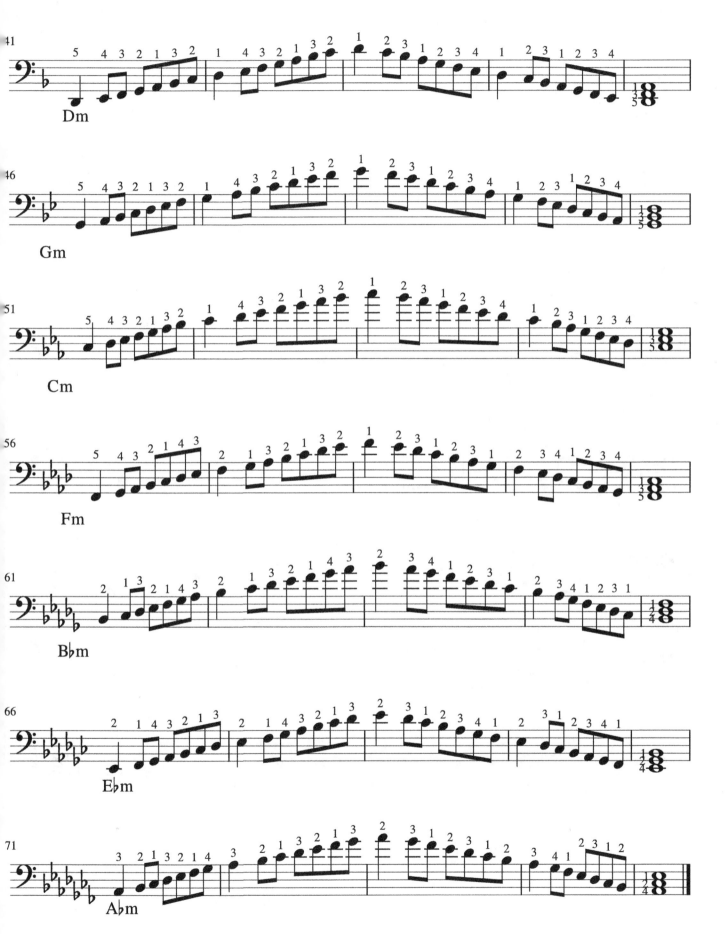

MAJOR CHORDS EXERCISES IN SHARP KEYS.

Piotr Tadrzyński

5. <u>MAJOR CHORDS</u> EXERCISES IN FLAT KEYS.

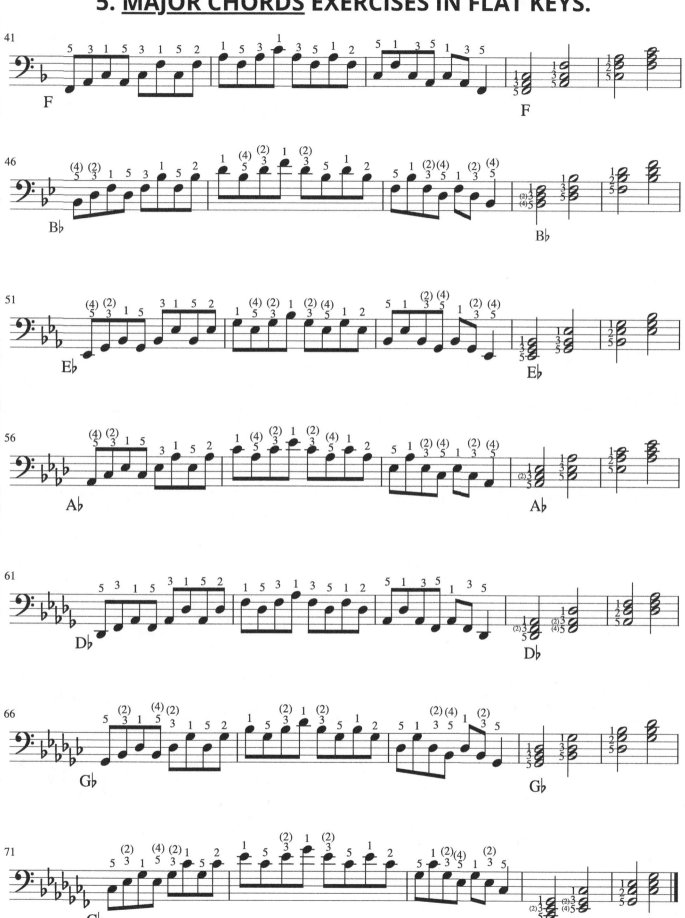

MINOR CHORDS EXERCISES IN SHARP KEYS.

Piotr Tadrzyński

MINOR CHORDS EXERCISES IN FLAT KEYS.

6. <u>MAJOR ARPEGGIOS</u> EXERCISES IN SHARP KEYS.

Piotr Tadrzyński

MAJOR ARPEGGIOS EXERCISES IN FLAT KEYS.

MINOR ARPEGGIOS EXERCISES IN SHARP KEYS.

Piotr Tadrzyński

MINOR ARPEGGIOS EXERCISES IN FLAT KEYS.

7. ALTERNATING EXERCISE SHARP KEYS FOR BOTH HANDS.

Piotr Tadrzyński

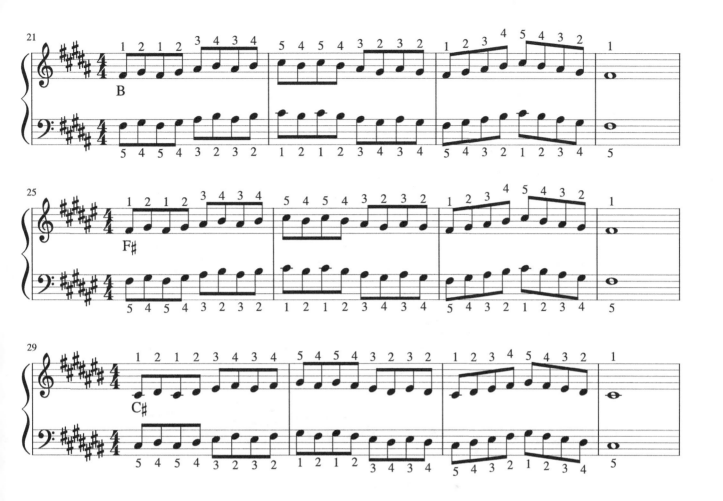

ALTERNATING EXERCISE FLAT KEYS FOR BOTH HANDS.

8. Styles Based on Progression Chords C-Am-Em-G for Patterns.

All accompaniment styles will be based on the sample chord progression **I-vi-iii-V** **(C-Am-Em-G)**. This is just an example progression and the styles shown in the book will fit any other progression as well. The styles demonstrated in the book are for the left hand, but they can also be combined with the right hand and freely mixed, as shown at the end of this book. However, I would like to focus on the left hand as it is usually responsible for creating the accompaniment, while the right hand will focus more on melody or chord playing.

Example below:

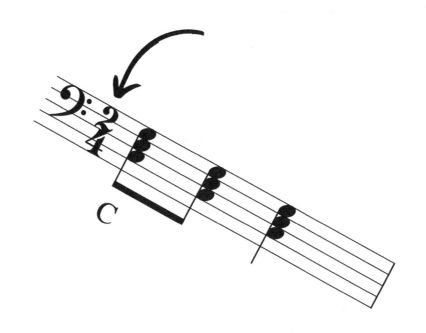

9. <u>100</u> Accompaniment Patterns in <u>2/4 Meter.</u>

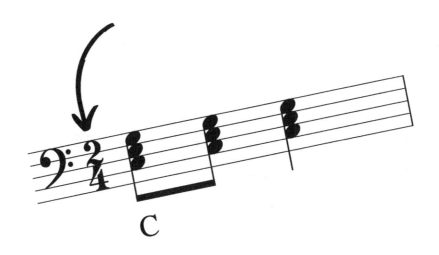

9.1. <u>CHORDAL</u> ACCOMPANIMENT.

9.2. BASIC ACCOMPANIMENT.

9.3. <u>FIGURED</u> ACCOMPANIMENT.

24

9.3. FIGURED ACCOMPANIMENT.

25

9.3. FIGURED ACCOMPANIMENT.

9.3. <u>FIGURED</u> ACCOMPANIMENT.

27

9.3. **<u>FIGURED</u> ACCOMPANIMENT.**

28

9.3. <u>FIGURED</u> ACCOMPANIMENT.

9.3. <u>FIGURED</u> ACCOMPANIMENT.

30

9.3. FIGURED ACCOMPANIMENT.

9.3. <u>FIGURED</u> ACCOMPANIMENT.

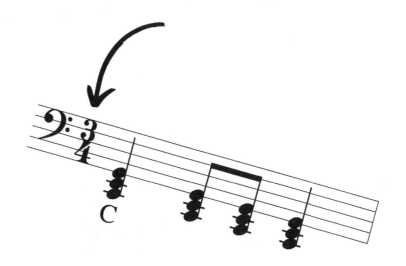

10. **100** Accompaniment Patterns in **3/4 Meter.**

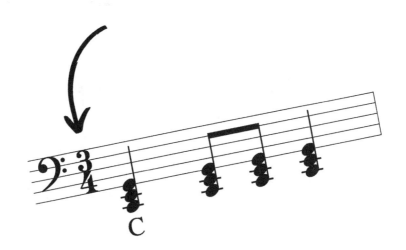

10.1. CHORDAL ACCOMPANIMENT.

34

10.1. <u>CHORDAL</u> ACCOMPANIMENT.

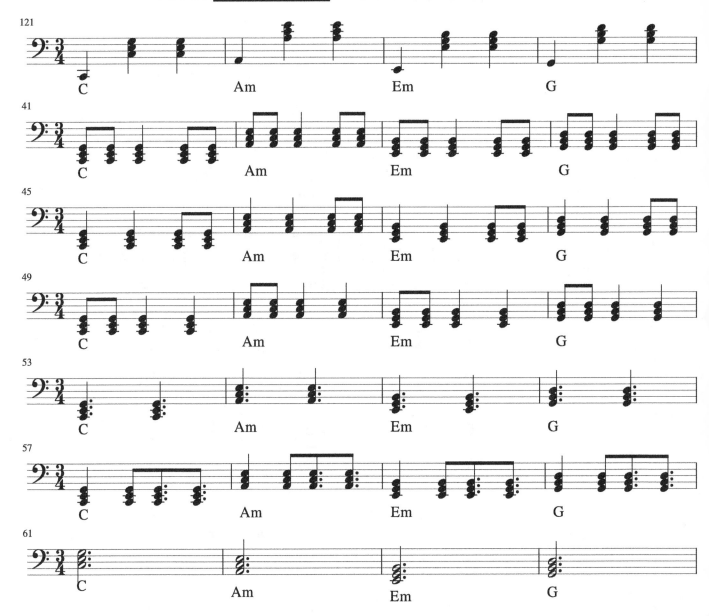

10.2. <u>BASIC</u> ACCOMPANIMENT.

10.3. <u>FIGURED</u> ACCOMPANIMENT.

10.3. <u>FIGURED</u> ACCOMPANIMENT.

10.3. **<u>FIGURED</u>** ACCOMPANIMENT.

39

10.3. <u>FIGURED</u> ACCOMPANIMENT.

10.3. <u>FIGURED</u> ACCOMPANIMENT.

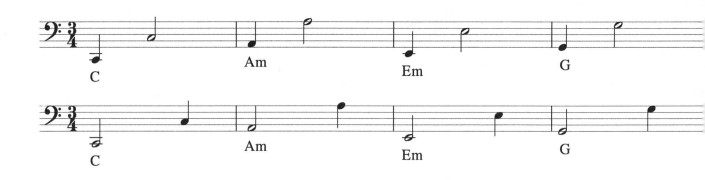

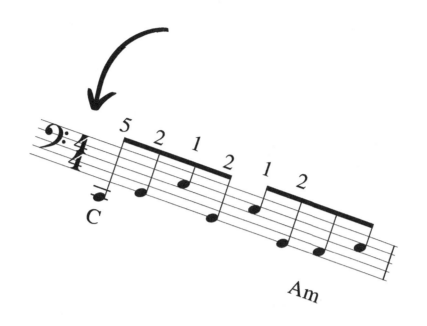

11. <u>100</u> Accompaniment Patterns in <u>**4/4 Meter.**</u>

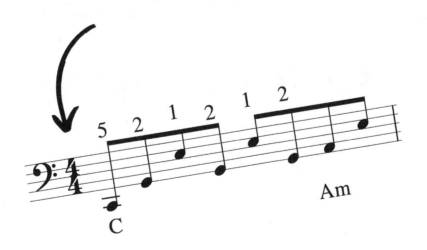

11.1. <u>CHORDAL</u> ACCOMPANIMENT.

11.2. <u>BASIC</u> ACCOMPANIMENT.

11.3. <u>FIGURED</u> ACCOMPANIMENT.

11.3. **FIGURED** ACCOMPANIMENT.

11.3. FIGURED ACCOMPANIMENT.

11.3. <u>FIGURED</u> ACCOMPANIMENT.

11.3. **FIGURED** ACCOMPANIMENT.

11.3. <u>FIGURED</u> ACCOMPANIMENT.

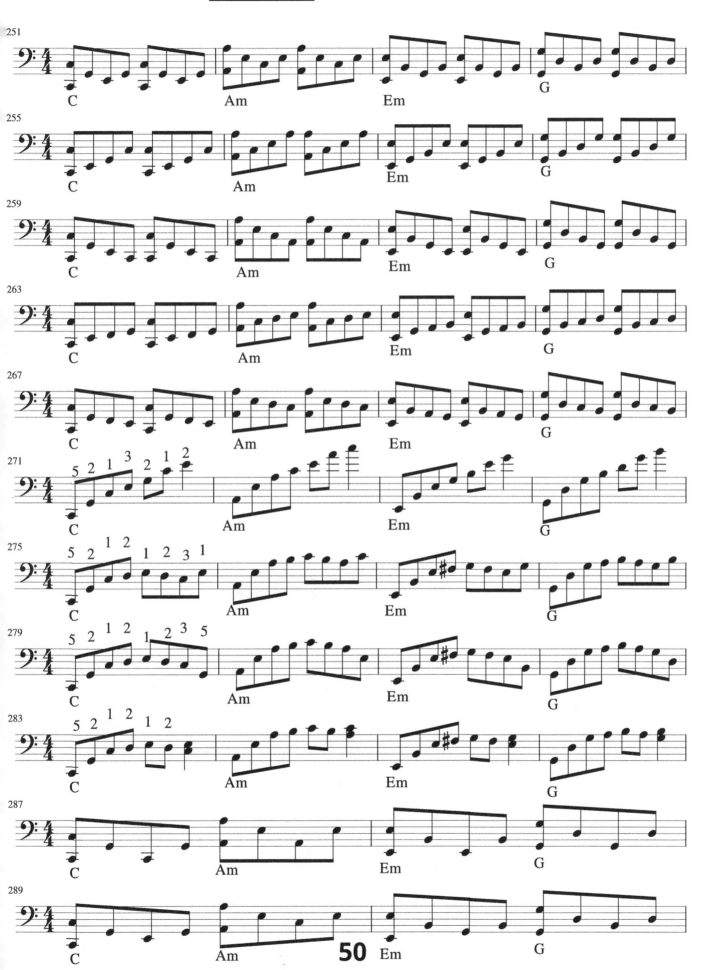

50

11.3. FIGURED ACCOMPANIMENT.

51

11.3. <u>FIGURED</u> ACCOMPANIMENT.

11.3. **FIGURED** ACCOMPANIMENT.

12. <u>ACCOMPANIMENT FOR RIGHT HAND.</u>

THE MOST POPULAR ACCOMPANIMENT STYLES FOR THE RIGHT HAND

Piotr Tadrzyński

13. ACCOMPANIMENT FOR BOTH HANDS.

THE MOST POPULAR ACCOMPANIMENT STYLES FOR THE BOTH HANDS!

14. HOW TO CREATE ACCOMPANIMENT ON YOUR OWN BASED ON THE ABOVE PATTERNS.

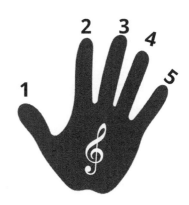

When combining both hands in piano accompaniment, it is important to choose the appropriate pattern for the left hand. The pattern for the right hand should also be selected, even from the above-mentioned schemes. It is crucial that both patterns are in the same meter. The right hand can even improvise a simple melody, thus creating an interesting improvisation that can also serve as accompaniment.

One effective method is to start by playing chords in the left hand using a basic accompaniment pattern while playing the melody with the right hand. Once you feel comfortable, try incorporating more complex patterns in the left hand, such as figuration accompaniment, to add depth and complexity to the accompaniment.

It is also important to consider the harmony and rhythm of the piece when choosing patterns for the left hand. For example, when playing a fast-paced piece, using a simpler pattern in the left hand may be more effective to avoid overwhelming the melody. On the other hand, a slower piece may benefit from a more intricate pattern in the left hand to fill the sound.

Ultimately, finding the right balance between both hands requires practice and experimentation. It is important to try out different combinations of patterns and rhythms for the left and right hand until you find a combination that fits well with the melody and overall style of the piece.

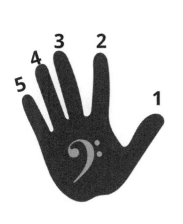

58

15. SUMMARY ACCOMPANIMENT BOOK.

The meters **2/4, 3/4,** and **4/4** are the most commonly used meters in music. We hav built over **300** different accompaniment patterns based on these meters. With them, yo will be able to play a single piece in many different ways. The accompaniment pattern are universal and can be used with any chord progression. This book definitely help develop piano playing skills and create beautiful accompaniments.

Personally, I recommend mixing the styles included in this book, which means choosing style for the left hand and trying to play every possible style in the right hand, and vic versa. The number of combinations of such styles and mixing them in both hands i endless, but the key to success is time and practice. The more you play and practice th styles, the better combination you will choose for yourself. It is important to remembe that the combined styles should be in the same meter.

All accompaniment styles can also be applied to any song or melody and even used fo **improvisation**.

SEE OUR OTHER PRODUCTS!

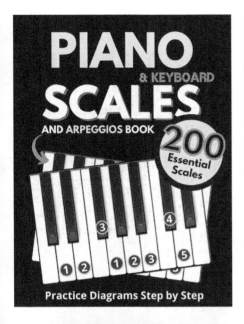

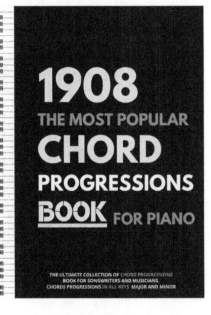

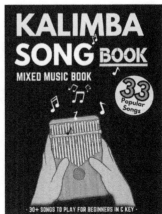

QR CODES TO MY PRODUCTS

USE QR CODES AND VISIT ME:

Summary, this book delves deep into various interesting styles of accompaniment for both the left and right hand, showcasing many exciting possibilities that you can practically apply in your daily playing. It serves as a valuable source of information for pianists who want to better understand accompaniment, improvisation, and the principles of selecting accompaniment styles for different pieces. If you have read this book and find it valuable, I encourage you to leave a review below. Your feedback is important to me as it helps me create new content that better meets the needs of readers. Finally, I would like to remind you that below are QR codes that will take you to my training platform and social media pages where you can find more information and resources on music theory and learning to play instruments.

https://muzycznelekcje.pl/

Thank you for your purchase and I wish you rapid progress in your playing!

Made in the USA
Las Vegas, NV
23 December 2024

15206706R00037